I0707155

THE BOOK OF 333 QUESTIONS

by J.L. Brown

Also by J.L. Brown

111 Journal Prompts for Self Discovery
1st Edition, 2019

Book of 333 Questions by J.L. Brown
1st Edition
Self-published
Kindle Direct Publishing

© Copyright 2020 by J.L. Brown

All rights reserved.

No part of this publication may be reproduced,
stored in a retrieval system, stored in a database
and / or published in any form or by any means,
electronic, mechanical, photocopying, recording or
otherwise, without the prior written permission of
the publisher.

"It's not always in the answers, but in the
pondering of the questions that you find what
you're looking for."

xo J.L. Brown

The Book of 333 Questions is designed to be playful and inquisitive. It's uses are endless!

Ask yourself. Ask your partner. Ask your family. Ask your friends.

Bring this book to game night. Leave it on the coffee table. Refer to it as a source of conversational inspiration!

Answer freely, openly, and honestly with whatever comes to mind first.

Allow your answers and the conversations around them to evolve.

Think. Laugh. Play. Expand. Have fun!

Share some of your favorites with us on the interwebs.

 XOJLBrown

Thank you. Thank you. Thank you!

1.   What is one of the most spontaneous things you have ever done?

2.   What did you want to be when you were a kid?

3.   What is one of your most embarrassing memories?

4.   What does love mean to you?

5.   How might you behave differently tomorrow if you won one hundred million dollars tonight?

6.   What do you aspire to be in life?

7.   What would you do if you were not afraid?

8.   What are your fears?

9.   What kind of impact do you intend to make in our world?

10.   What is a lofty dream of yours?

11.   When do you feel the most vulnerable?

12.   Do you believe in Karma? Why or why not?

13.   What are your thoughts on theories that suggest multiple realities?

14.   What never fails to make you smile?

15.   What was the last thing that moved you to tears?

16.   In your opinion, what does it mean to be human?

17.   What are you grateful for that you often take for granted?

18.   What is your most unpopular opinion?

19.   Are you a dog person, a cat person, or both?

20.   If you could shapeshift into any real or mythical creature at your own command, what would you choose and why?

21.   You can master one superpower of your choice. What do you choose?

22.   If you could be the opposite sex for one full day, how would you spend your day?

23.   What has been your favorite travel experience to date?

24.   Where do you want to travel that you have not yet been?

25.   How is your relationship with money and finances?

26.   Do you believe in luck? Why or why not?

27.   Do you believe in miracles? Why or why not?

28.   What are some of your favorite *not-so-good* things to indulge in?

29.   You have been offered a chance to stay on a secluded island by yourself for one month. At the end of the month you will receive a reward of twenty five thousand dollars. You will not have access to modern technology or the internet. Do you accept the offer? Why or why not?

30.   *(See above question)* If you replied yes, you can bring five personal items with you. What do you bring?

31.   Which musical instrument would you *easily* like to master?

32.   Which would you prefer: an all-inclusive cruise through the Bahamas, or a backpacking trip through the Himalaya Mountains?

33.   What is your favorite form of art and why?

34.   What societal changes would you like to see
       projected into our collective future?

35.   What do you wish someone would have told you
       when you were a child?

36.   What is one of your favorite childhood
       memories?

37.   Do you have any regrets? If so, what are they?

38.   If you could change one thing about your
       current life, what would it be?

39.   Have you ever been / are you in love? What is it
       like?

40.   What are the first three things you do when you
       wake up in the morning?

41.   What are the last three things you do before you go to sleep at night?

42.   You have one full day with no obligations, plenty of money in the bank, and nobody else to tend to. What do you do?

43.   You have ten dollars in your bank account until Friday. It's Tuesday. How do you spend it?

44.   Which is your favorite season and why?

45.   Housing: rent or buy? Why?

46.   Coffee or tea?

47.   What is your all time favorite meal?

48.   What is your favorite dessert?

49.   What is the last dream you remember having?

50.   What are your thoughts on abortion?

51.   Do you want to raise children? Why or why not?

52.   Would you ever / have you ever done a fitness
       race of any kind?

53.   Have you ever considered joining the Peace
       Corps?

54.   Who, out of all your friends, do you think would
       make the best leader?

55.   What are some of your personal unique gifts and
       innate skill sets?

56.   Do you feel you have a particular purpose in
       life? If so, what is it?

57.   What are your thoughts on universal healthcare?

58.   What are your thoughts on homelessness?

59.   What are your thoughts on the Law of Attraction (*thoughts become things, like attracts like*) and manifestation?

60.   What is your favorite cocktail?

61.   Wine or beer?

62.   Have you or someone you know been affected by the opioid epidemic? Tell me more.

63.   What are your thoughts on addiction?

64.   Who is the most interesting person you know? Tell me about him/her.

65.   What do you find sexy?

66.   Have you ever volunteered your time and skills to people or organizations in need? If so, tell me about your experience.

67.   You can pass one bill into federal law. No questions asked. No resistance from anybody. What law do you create and why?

68.   How do you hope our national and global politics will shift in the next 5-10 years?

69.   You are broke. A billionaire offers to donate one million dollars in your name to any charitable cause(s) of your choice. In return, you are to spend six weeks as a volunteer at an orphanage in Tibet. Do you accept the offer? Why or why not?

70.   In your opinion, what is the best thing about our current information age and the coming of the internet?

71.   In your opinion, what is the worst thing about our current information age and the coming of the internet?

72.   In your opinion, what is the best thing about social media?

73.   In your opinion, what is the worst thing about social media?

74.   You have agreed to spend one month in total solitude for fifty thousand dollars. Your choices are between a cabin in the woods, a cabin in the mountains, or a hut on the beach. Which do you choose and why?

75.   You can ask one question to any one person, dead or alive. What and who do you ask?

76.   (*See above question*) What do you think their answer might be?

77.   You have to flee your country due to unforeseen issues. Where do you go and why?

78.   A genie comes to grant you three wishes. You cannot wish for more wishes. You cannot bring anyone back from the dead. And you cannot make anyone fall in love. What are your three wishes?

79.   What are your top three personal values?

80.   Why do you think they call it "falling in love"?

81.   What has been your biggest accomplishment in life so far?

82.   What do you think happens when we die?

83.   Have you ever had someone close to you die? If so, how has that changed your perspective on life?

84.   Do you believe aliens exist?

85.   What would you do if you came into contact with an alien?

86.   If you could, would you go to Mars?

87.   Do you believe there are ghosts / spirits amongst us?

88.   Have you ever seen or come into contact with a ghost / spirit?

89.   If you could send one musical artist or group, dead or alive, into space to perform a song or album as a representation of humans on Earth, who would you send and why? Which song or album?

90.   What is one of your favorite quotes?

91.   What is your muse?

92.   You are driving down a busy street and notice a small dog running towards oncoming traffic ahead of you. What do you do?

93.   Do you believe in God? Why or why not?

94.   You find an envelope on the ground at a busy train station with one thousand dollars in it. What do you do?

95.   What is your earliest memory?

96.   Did you have an imaginary friend as a child? If so, tell me about him/her.

97.   How old were you when you had your first kiss? What was it like?

98.   What similarities do you share with your parents?

99.   What differences do you have with your parents?

100.   What were some of your favorite childhood games to play?

101.   What are some of your current favorite games to play?

102.   What were some of your favorite childhood movies and TV shows to watch?

103.   What are some of your current favorite movies and TV shows to watch?

104.   A friend of yours needs a kidney to live. You are healthy and able to provide, with minimal risk. What do you do?

105.   (*See above question*) What if it was for a friend of a friend, a stranger?

106.   Do you have siblings? If so, tell me about them. If not, what was it like being an only child?

107.   Apple or Android? Why?

108.   When did you stop believing in Santa Claus and The Tooth Fairy?

109.   What is your favorite holiday and why?

110.   Who raised you? How has this shaped you as a
        person?

111.   What is something that you have always wanted
        to do but have not yet had the opportunity to do it?

112.   What do you appreciate most about yourself?

113.   Who is your oldest friend? What do you love
        about this person?

114.   Are you afraid of death? Why or why not?

115.   What are your thoughts on religion?

116.   What are your thoughts on spirituality?

117.   Are you a religious / spiritual person?

118.   What are your thoughts on our current national and global politics?

119.   What kind of world do you hope to create for our future generations to thrive in?

120.   How do you think other people view you?

121.   Do you feel understood by your family and friends?

122.   What do you wish others understood better about you?

123.   What recreational drugs have you tried? What did you hate? What did you like?

124.   What are your thoughts on American culture?

125.   Do you (want to) know how to shoot a gun?

126.   What will you do in the case of a zombie apocalypse?

127.   There is a costume party you are attending in three weeks. A homemade costume is mandatory. What do you show up as?

128.   Do you believe you create your own reality? Explain.

129.   What are your thoughts on reincarnation?

130.   Do you have any memories or hunches from past lives you may have lived?

131.   Do you enjoy spending time alone? Why or why not?

132.   How do you spend your time alone?

133.   What household chore do you dislike the most?

134.   What is your ideal social setting?

135.   When you are having a shitty day, what do you
do to cheer yourself up?

136.   What is your favorite kind of music to dance to?

137.   When and who was your first concert? Who
were you with?

138.   What is one of your favorite books, and why?

139.   You recently won over half a billion dollars in
the lottery and were unable to remain anonymous,
so you've decided to change your name. What do
you change it to?

140.   How do you express your emotions?

141.   What is your silliest pet peeve?

142. What do you do everyday to take care of yourself?

143. Would you consider yourself to be an organized person?

144. What words of wisdom can you share with our collective youth?

145. What do you know to be true?

146. Do you believe in soulmates? Twin flames? Explain.

147. Have you ever met a soulmate or twin flame? If so, how did you know and what was it like?

148. What do you think is on the other side of a Black Hole?

149. How do you manage high levels of stress?

150.   In this present moment, how do you feel?

151.   In this present moment, what are you most grateful for?

152.   What mistakes have you made that you have not forgiven yourself for?

153.   Do you hold a grudge towards anybody who has done you wrong?

154.   (*See above question*) If so, do you think you could ever forgive this person? Why or why not?

155.   What is a particularly difficult obstacle you have overcome?

156.   (*See above question*) How did you overcome it?

157.   What do you take a lot of pride in?

158.   What is one of the bravest things you've ever done?

159.   What is one of the bravest things you've ever witnessed?

160.   Have you ever witnessed a miracle? If so, tell me more.

161.   In your opinion, what changes could be made in our current public school systems to better prepare our youth and create a brighter future?

162.   Do you think it's possible that we are living in a hologram? Why or why not?

163.   Blue Pill or Red Pill?

164.   What secrets do you have that you are willing to share?

165.   Have you ever thought about joining the military? Why or why not?

166.   Who do you wish you could see on a more regular basis?

167.   If you could go back in time for one day, where and when would you go and why?

168.   How is your relationship with yourself? Do you love yourself? Do you take care of yourself? Do you make yourself a priority?

169.   How do you feel about your body?

170.   What are your thoughts on ancient Eastern medicine?

171.   What are your thoughts on witchcraft?

172.   Are you generally a skeptic or believer of new-age materials? Explain.

173.   Do you have, or do you know anybody that has, psychic or supernatural abilities? If so, tell me more!

174.   What is it like being you?

175.   What would make your life more enjoyable in this present moment?

176.   When was the last time you were really angry about something?

177.   When was the last time you were nervous / excited about something?

178.   When was the last time you cried?

179.   When was the last time you cried in public?

180.   When was the last time you laughed so hard you cried?

181.   What would you say to someone who is currently going through a difficult time?

182.   What do you have an irrational fear of?

183.   Have you ever driven or ridden on a motorcycle?

184.   What makes humans special?

185.   What makes you weird / different from most others?

186.   Who do you go to when you need advice? Why?

187.   Who have been / are your greatest mentors?

188.   When you get great news, who do you tell first?

189.   When was the last time you did something just for the joy of doing it? What did you do?

190.   Who is / are your best friend(s)?

191.   How do you stay connected with your loved
        ones?

192.   Where are you from?

193.   What is your favorite thing about your
        hometown?

194.   Do you still live in / visit your hometown?

195.   How has your hometown shaped you as a
        person?

196.   What sets you apart from the rest of your
        family?

197.   What do you enjoy learning about?

198. You are to nominate someone to speak on a topic intended to inspire thousands of people. Who do you nominate and why?

199. You are to nominate someone to receive a total make-over and a new chance at life. Who do you nominate and why?

200. In your opinion, who are some of the most talented musicians, artists, actors, and actresses of our time?

201. In your opinion, what are some of the best movies to date?

202. In this present moment, are you happy?

203. What is something that you really wanted and received?

204. Have you ever been told you look like a celebrity? If so, who?

205.   Have you ever wanted to be an actor or actress?
Musician? Model? Artist?

206.   Do you generally prefer to go out or stay in?

207.   Who was the last person you hugged?

208.   If you could be someone else for one day, who
would you be and why?

209.   What has been one of your greatest adventures
to date?

210.   If someone really wanted to impress you with a
gift, what might they get you?

211.   What does your ideal date night entail?

212.   In your opinion, what are some of the most
important aspects of a healthy relationship?

213. What is the most effective way for someone to show you they love you? What is your "love language"?

214. How do you show love to others?

215. What is the best thing about being in an intimate relationship?

216. What is the most challenging thing about being in an intimate relationship?

217. What do you think makes you a good partner?

218. What do you need from your partner to feel connected and loved?

219. What would you say is your greatest strength?

220. What would you say is your greatest weakness?

221.   If given the opportunity, would you go on a
        spaceship ride around Earth?

222.   What are your thoughts on crop circles?

223.   Who was your first crush?

224.   Would you ever consider going vegetarian or
        vegan? Why or why not?

225.   What is your favorite way to exercise your
        body?

226.   What has been your best year to date, and why?

227.   What might you do differently if you could
        relive this past year?

228.   Do you gamble? Why or why not?

229.   In life, are you more of a risk taker or do you
        prefer to play it safe?

230.   Do you have / want any pets? If so, what do you have / want?

231.   What is your desired personal style?

232.   In your opinion, what makes someone a good friend?

233.   When was the last time you spoke / spent time with your best friend(s)?

234.   Do you have / want any tattoos? If so, what are they?

235.   Do you have / want any piercings? If so, what are they?

236.   What do you want to be when you grow up?

237.   What are your thoughts on war?

238.   Do you believe there will ever be peace on
       Earth? Why or why not?

239.   What do you think it will take to experience
       peace on Earth?

240.   In your opinion, in what ways can we work
       individually and collectively to create a more
       peaceful future?

241.   What are your thoughts on racism?

242.   What do you think the evolution of technology
       will look like in ten years? Twenty years? Fifty
       years?

243.   What cultures do you find to be some of the
       most fascinating, and why?

244.   Have you ever been the minority in a room?

245.   Have you ever been to a therapist? If so, how
       was your experience?

246.   What does your ideal night out with friends look like?

247.   Have you ever taken a road trip? What's been your favorite?

248.   What epic road trip do you want to embark on but haven't been able to yet?

249.   (*See above question*) What do you need to make that happen?

250.   Have you ever had your heart broken? How did it feel?

251.   What has acted as a catalyst for change in your life?

252.   Who can you tell absolutely anything to without fear of judgement?

253.   What has always been true about you?

254.   What do others usually like about you?

255.   Are you more of an introvert or an extrovert?

256.   Would you consider yourself to be highly
        intuitive / empathic?

257.   What is the most valuable thing you own?

258.   What can someone expect when they come into
        your personal space?

259.   What do you often daydream about?

260.   What do you want to happen with your body
        when you die?

261.   What TV show series have you watched all the
        way through, more than once?

262.   How do you find ways to connect and relate to others who are very different from you?

263.   Which languages do you know fluently?

264.   (*See above question*) What other languages would you like to know fluently?

265.   What do you think the experience of death is like?

266.   How do you hope to die?

267.   You can take yourself and five other people on an all expenses paid one week vacation anywhere in the world. Where do you go and who do you take?

268.   Your most recent ex called and wants to grab a coffee. Do you go?

269.   Which do you prefer: sweet or savory?

270.   What are your thoughts on the cost and access to higher academic education?

271.   What are your thoughts on credit / debt?

272.   Have you ever experienced *deja vu*?

273.   What are your thoughts on *deja vu*?

274.   You have plans to get drinks with your best friend tonight. You are on your way out any minute. Your significant other calls you crying because they just got fired at work. What do you do?

275.   You have a fear of heights. Your friends call to invite you on a beautiful local hiking adventure with spectacular views. "Totally doable, even for a novice like yourself!", they promise. Do you go? Why or why not?

276.   What can you do today that your future self will thank you for tomorrow and onward?

277. What do you appreciate the most about where you currently live?

278. What is something you would like to change about yourself?

279. Who is someone that you admire? What do you admire about this person?

280. In your opinion, what does it mean to be a good person?

281. Who has inspired you to be a better person? How so?

282. What do you think makes *you* a good person?

283. How do you feel about getting older?

284. What is the best part about getting older?

285. What is the worst part about getting older?

286.   If you could live forever, would you?

287.   How long do you want to live?

288.   Have / would you ever consider fostering or
        adopting a child?

289.   What 'social norms' or 'social rules' do you find
        to be ridiculous and unreasonable?

290.   What do you look for when making new
        friends?

291.   What do you look for in a partner?

292.   What do you think makes *you* a good friend?

293.   What do you think makes *you* a good partner?

294.   In your opinion, who has the sexiest accent?

295. You can see any music artist or band from throughout history live in concert. Who do you go see, and when?

296. In this present moment, what is on your mind?

297. What is a cataclysmic event from your life that has changed you in a big way?

298. What day from your past would you love to relive again? Tell me about it.

299. Hindsight is 20/20. What words of wisdom do you have for your ten year younger self?

300. What is something most people wouldn't know about you?

301. What major city in the world do you think matches your personality best?

302.   Remember a time you witnessed an injustice as a bystander. How did you feel and what did you do?

303.   Do you prefer the fast route or the scenic route?

304.   Where did you think you would be today, ten years ago?

305.   Where did you think you would be today, five years ago?

306.   Where did you think you would be today, one year ago?

307.   How do you feel about where you are in life right this moment?

308.   Where do you see yourself in one year from today?

309.   Where do you see yourself in five years from today?

310.   Where do you see yourself in ten years from today?

311.   How do you make decisions about what to do next in life?

312.   If someone were to make a movie about you, what would it be called? What is the plot?

313.   If you could live in a different time period, past or future, which would you pick and why?

314.   What do you think the world will be like in the year 2120?

315.   If you had to live the life of an animal, which animal would you pick and why?

316.   Do you believe in love at first sight? Why or why not?

317.   Have you ever been in love with someone you
        could not be with?

318.   Who is your favorite comedian and why?

319.   Do you like theme parks and roller coasters?
        Why or why not?

320.   When was the last time you were on a roller
        coaster?

321.   What does ultimate freedom mean to you?

322.   Do you believe that everything happens for a
        reason? Why or why not?

323.   Do you believe in fate or destiny? Why or why
        not?

324.   What are your thoughts on free will in regards
        to fate or destiny?

325.   In your opinion, which decade from the 1900's had the best style?

326.   In your opinion, which decade from the 1900's had the best music?

327.   What advice do you have for someone who just got out of a long-term relationship?

328.   Who was the last person you said "I love you" to?

329.   Tell me about a time when you felt happy and free. Who were you with? What were you doing? How did it feel?

330.   What little things do you do everyday that help make the world a better place?

331.   In your opinion, what is the most exciting thing about being alive?

332.   What entails a perfect yet mundane day for you?

333.   What question(s) do you hate being asked the
      most?

*"The important thing is not to stop questioning.
Curiosity has its own reason for existence. One
cannot help but be in awe when he contemplates
the mysteries of eternity, of life, of the marvelous
structure of reality. It is enough if one tries merely
to comprehend a little of this mystery each day.
Never lose a holy curiosity."*

—*Albert Einstein*
From the memoirs of William Miller, an editor,
quoted in Life magazine, May 2, 1955;
Expanded, p. 281.
With permission:
The Hebrew University of Jerusalem

www.ingramcontent.com/pod-product-compliance
Lightning Source LLC
Chambersburg PA
CBHW050702250726
48662CB00002B/793